Sketching Outdoors in Autumn

Young
Red Squirrel
drawn actual size
OCT 17, 1987

ALSO BY JIM ARNOSKY

Deer at the Brook

Drawing from Nature

Drawing Life in Motion

Flies in the Water, Fish in the Air:
A Personal Introduction to Fly Fishing

Freshwater Fish & Fishing

Gray Boy

Raccoons and Ripe Corn

Secrets of a Wildlife Watcher

Sketching Outdoors in Spring

Sketching Outdoors in Summer

Sketching Outdoors in Winter

Watching Foxes

wild ducks
from recollected
sighting (naked eye)
Jim Arnosky
1987

Sketching Outdoors in Autumn

BY JIM ARNOSKY

LOTHROP, LEE & SHEPARD BOOKS   NEW YORK

This season is dedicated to
Phil Emerson—
big, strong, full of vinegar,
and taken in his prime.

Copyright © 1988 by Jim Arnosky

All rights reserved. No part of this book may be reproduced or utilized in any form or by any means, electronic or mechanical, including photocopying, recording or by any information storage and retrieval system, without permission in writing from the Publisher. Inquiries should be addressed to Lothrop, Lee & Shepard Books, a division of William Morrow & Company, Inc., 105 Madison Avenue, New York, New York 10016. Printed in the United States of America.

First Edition 1 2 3 4 5 6 7 8 9 10

Library of Congress Cataloging in Publication Data

Arnosky, Jim. Sketching outdoors in autumn / by Jim Arnosky.   p.   cm.   ISBN 0-688-06288-1 : 1. Outdoor life in art —Juvenile literature. 2. Animals in art—Juvenile literature. 3. Plants in art—Juvenile literature. 4. Wildlife art—Juvenile literature. 5. Landscape in art—Juvenile literature. 6. Autumn in art—Juvenile literature. 7. Drawing—Technique—Juvenile literature.   I. Title

NC825.O88A74 1988 743.83—dc19   88-1244 CIP AC

INTRODUCTION

"Who painted the first picture on a bone
in the caves of France? A hunter."
ALDO LEOPOLD
from his essay "Goose Music"

In setting out to do these outdoor sketches, I followed my own hunting instincts, hoping they would put me on the track of an autumn beyond the spectacular show of colorful leaves: a pencil sketcher's season, with interesting lines, sharp contrasts, and a variety of tones. I found what I was looking for in the animals' autumn, which is wild, robust, and often raw.

Much of the time I spent in the forested mountains six miles north of my home. With sketch pad and portable easel, I rambled in my truck over logging roads, hiked along rocky ridges, and sloshed through swampy hollows. Everywhere I found animal tracks and signs. Sometimes I found the animals themselves and sketched them on the spot.

Whenever I came down out of the mountains, I retained a wild viewpoint, always skirting the edges of farms and villages, sketching in quiet cornfields, windy meadows, and old, forgotten orchards.

Except for the two weeks of deer season, when I avoided the woods for fear of being accidentally shot, I went out every day to sketch. I especially liked going forth the day after a rain, when the fallen leaves were soaked and softened and I could walk silently on them. To my mind, stealth was all-important. The autumn I was hunting had to be tracked and stalked before it could be captured.

Jim Arnosky
Ramtails
Autumn 1987

THIS IS A CLEAR MOUNTAIN LAKE that I know better than anyone else does. I've explored most of its shoreline on foot and most of its water while wading or in my canoe.

On summer evenings I fish here for yellow perch, smallmouth bass, and rainbow trout. In September I come less to fish and more to sit and watch the season change. Because of the high elevation, autumn arrives here earlier than it does down in the valleys. It blows in from the north.

One crisp September afternoon I set up my easel on a small beach and, facing the water and the wind, sketched autumn coming.

Patches of drifted foam along a shoreline indicate that shore is leeward.

To make the rocks in my sketch look wave-washed clean, I used sharp, clear outlines to draw them.

By carefully drawing water waves, making them gradually smaller as they get farther away, you can create a sense of depth. In this sketch I squeezed a mile of lake onto eight inches of paper.

9

One night I was driving home from the lake and a bull moose stepped out onto the road ahead of me. The moose had a huge rack of antlers and distinctive white legs. I watched the moose cross the road and then disappear back into the dark forest.

The next morning I returned to the spot and located the moose's tracks. After crossing the road, the bull walked through the woods to an open, marshy area. There he followed a narrow, meandering brook. In the wet ground the moose's tracks were sloppy and misshapen. I found one print that was pressed neatly and began to draw it.

The impression was a few inches deep, and all around it the black mud was fractured. The longer I looked at the large hoofprint, the more I felt the presence of its maker. Every few minutes I looked up from my work and scanned the marsh to assure myself that I was indeed alone.

Drawing an animal's footprint can be as interesting and challenging as drawing the animal itself.

When you draw a footprint, start by sketching the overall shape of the impression. Next shade in the print's deepest plane, completing hard shadows first, then adding softer shadows.

Work upward and out of the print, shading different levels, until you have filled in your initial outline.

Notice any small twigs, leaves, and pebbles that may have been smashed down into the print by the maker's foot. Add these things to your sketch, each with its proper shading.

Bull Moose Track
Actual Size
Jim Arnosky
Sept, 1987

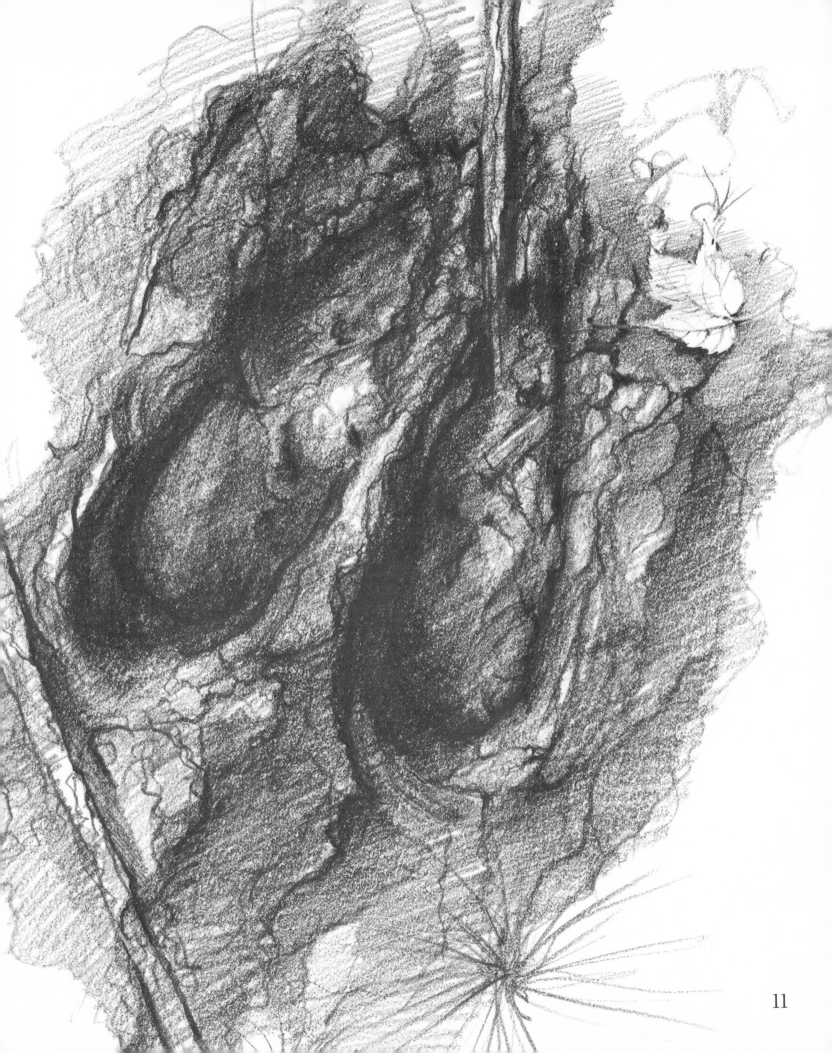

Notice the way a deer gracefully moves its neck. The long neck, a key feature of deer anatomy, must be studied before you can draw deer accurately.

White-tailed Deer
in the forest —
Drawn from nature
Jim Arnosky
Sept. '87

A few days later, not far from where I had seen the moose, I spotted two deer, both does. They were feeding in a swath cut in the forest by loggers. It had been raining all morning, and the woods were dripping wet. The ground was soaked and soft. I was able to crawl silently from downwind to within seventy-five feet of the deer.

One doe was mostly hidden from my view. The other was in the open. I stayed crouched low and began to sketch her. Still feeding, she began walking toward me. When she was about fifty feet away, she stopped and looked up, eyeballing me directly. Then, to my surprise, she started coming closer.

I continued to sketch the deer as she came. Some raindrops dripped down from the trees, splattering on my drawing. Their patter alerted the doe and she froze. Then she suddenly leaped away. Her companion followed. I stood and stretched my legs and watched both deer bound through the forest and out of sight.

Before stalking an animal to sketch it, open your sketch pad to a fresh leaf of paper, ready to be drawn on. While stalking the animal, hold the white paper surface toward your body so the animal you are sneaking up on cannot see it. Most wild animals become alarmed at the sight of anything bright.

When you see animals in woods or fields, chances are their feet will be hidden by grasses, fallen leaves, or brush. When sketching an animal from life, draw its feet only if you can see them.

Autumn is the mating season for deer. During this time male deer are unpredictable. If this had been a buck approaching me, it could have been dangerous. I would have eased my way out of there instead of staying to sketch.

Grasshopper
chewing
my sketch pad

This sketch was done on a windy autumn afternoon in a wild meadow close to my home. Downy milkweed seeds were fluffing out of their pods and blowing away. Randomly, I chose one milkweed plant to sketch. Almost the moment I began, a grasshopper landed on the edge of my pad with a POP! and started chewing the soft paper.

The grasshopper chewed. I sketched. The wind plucked the milkweed seeds and carried them off to new places. When I sharpened my pencil, its shavings—lovely paper-thin curls of wood—became airborne and sailed downwind with the seeds.

Many of the plants you sketch during summer look quite different in fall, after they have gone to seed. When you go sketching outdoors in autumn, keep plants gone to seed in mind as seasonable drawing subjects.

In a sketch, a little detail can do wonders. Notice how I've actually detailed only a few of the seed heads in the white downy clusters.

Windborne seeds, so light and delicate, are produced by very coarse plants. This dichotomy is logical. A coarse, sturdy-stemmed plant resists the push of wind. This resistance provides purchase enabling the wind to pluck out the plant's light and airy seeds.

Milkweed
on a windy day

Jim Arnosky 1987

After the first hard frost, silage corn begins the slow process of curing in the field before it is cut and chopped into winter feed for cattle. This scene was sketched on two golden October days. The air was redolent with the vapors of drying corn. The corn plants were changing from green to yellow-tan. On the stalks the long, heavy ears of corn were just starting to droop.

It always takes me an extra long time to complete a sketch in an autumn cornfield. There is so much to look at. Every stalk, leaf, and ear is an individual study in aging.

I take notice of all the different types of fallen leaves on the ground around the cornfield and in between the corn rows.

Where there is woodland bordering the cornfield, I can't resist the temptation to leave my easel and go exploring.

It took me two whole afternoons to sketch this cornfield. If you must take more than one day to complete a scene, try to schedule subsequent sketching sessions at the same time of day, and on days when the weather is similar. Doing this will keep the light and shadows in your picture looking natural.

Gray Squirrel
eating corn
JEA Oct. 1987

When an animal is busy eating, it assumes a comfortable position and will probably stay still for a while. Take advantage and sketch away!

I spotted this gray squirrel as it was hopping from the cornfield, carrying a half ear of corn in its mouth. Once in the woods, the squirrel dropped the heavy ear and began removing the kernels one by one. Some corn kernels the squirrel ate; it buried others under the fallen leaves.

I sketched the squirrel while it was busy on the ground with the corn. When I attempted to move closer, the crackling of dry leaves underfoot gave me away. The squirrel abandoned the ear of corn and climbed a tree.

In the tree the squirrel struck a comical pose, balancing on a limb and nibbling a kernel it had carried up. After the squirrel had finished the piece of corn, it became agitated, shaking its tail angrily and scolding me with loud chipping noises. I waited to see if the squirrel would come back down to the ear of corn and resume feeding in front of me. But this was a wild squirrel, wary of people. It finally climbed higher up the tree and disappeared into some crotch or hole.

One morning, my coming to the cornfield interrupted a fox as it was burying a half-eaten mouse. I did not actually see the fox. I spotted a small, freshly dug hole at the base of a cornstalk, and near the rim of the tiny excavation were two fox pawprints. I must have startled the fox the moment it had dropped its food into the hole. No dirt at all had been pushed back down to cover the mouse. A fox usually covers its cache right away by pushing dirt over the cache with its nose.

Down in the tiny grave the mouse's fur looked clean and bright against the dark damp earth.

Sketch a hole in the ground the same way you would sketch a footprint. Begin by outlining the hole's circumference. Shade in the "floor" or deepest spot. Add shading on the walls of the hole. Then work on the ground around the hole's rim.

When sketching close-up views of earth, add all the ground detail such as leaf pieces, seeds, twigs, grasses, pebbles, and clumps of dirt.

Though I was tempted to reach into the hole and pick the mouse up so I could see it better to draw it, I did not. The mouse and the hole were the fox's private property.

looking down
into the hole
drawn actual size
CbA 1887

When sketching large and powerful animals from life, use bold, decisive strokes.

In a logged-over tract of forest land, I noticed a cow moose feeding on aspen saplings. After I had done two quick sketches of the moose, a second cow moose appeared from behind some brush. Then a third moose, also a cow, walked into view. Before I could catch my breath, a huge bull moose sauntered out of the nearby woods and joined the group. It was the white-legged bull I had seen at night on the forest road, four weeks earlier. In the daylight I estimated his weight at over a thousand pounds. His rack of antlers spread five feet across. Without question, I was in the presence of the King of Groton Forest!

Holding binoculars to my eyes with my left hand, I attempted to draw with my right. Both hands were trembling. I sketched as well as I could in my excited state, while the cows formed a single file and made their way up the sloping clearing. The bull followed closely behind them.

When you are sketching animals in the wild, stay crouched down, and the animals will be less apt to notice you.

Moose also mate in autumn. Bull moose are dangerous all the time, but during mating season they are extremely dangerous. To be safe, I stayed downwind from the moose and always more than two hundred feet away.

23

On a warm Indian summer day I followed moose tracks into one of the many swamps sunken into our mountains. It was late in the afternoon. The sun's rays angled across the swamp, lighting a row of tamarack trees on the far side. The tamarack needles were changed from their summer blue-green color to autumn gold. In the setting sunlight the tall slender trees glowed softly, like thick plumes of yellow smoke rising from the land.

I set up my easel and, standing in muddy moose tracks,
sketched the scene until lengthening shadows reached across
the swamp and extinguished the tamaracks' fire.

You never know what denizens may be hidden in a scene you are sketching. On my way out of the swamp, I saw a rare black lynx. It was also leaving the swamp. The lynx paused and looked at me, just long enough to send a shiver up my spine. Then the big cat padded silently into the shadowy forest.

I sketched this scene systematically, from the background forward, carefully leaving clean white paper where the bright tamaracks belonged. The darkly shaded foreground was drawn last.

Again on the trail of the moose, this time in high country, I came upon this macabre sight. At first glance I thought some animal had killed the grouse and carried it up the tree to eat it. But one striking bit of evidence pointed to the bizarre conclusion that the grouse had killed itself by flying head-on into the maple's slender trunk. The bird's neck had been broken by the impact.

The condition of the grouse's body, and other clues around the tree, suggested that the grouse was being chased through the air by a hawk and that, with the hawk coming fast upon it, the grouse had panicked, lost control, and smashed into the tree. The hawk had then perched on the fresh kill and characteristically skinned the grouse's underparts, including its legs. Swatches of skin with grouse feathers still attached lay about on the forest floor, along with both of the bird's detached wings. It appeared that the hawk had sought the choicest parts. Only the grouse's breast flesh and lungs had been eaten.

I walked around the tree, viewing the bird's carcass from many angles, looking beyond the horror, trying to see beauty in the hanging form. When I finally began sketching, I worked slowly and carefully to capture every telling detail—all the while thinking, not of death but of the life the grouse had lived, and of the life of the hunter it had fed.

Grouse feeding in a tree —
Groton Forest — JEA—Oct 1987

27

Deer still hunt
sketched from life
J.S.
Oct. 14, 198

I was driving through the woods, along a lumpy old railroad bed, when up ahead of me a deer dashed across the roadway. I stopped, shut off the truck's engine, and watched where the deer ran amid the hardwoods. About fifty feet from the road she came to an abrupt halt and stood perfectly camouflaged against the brown fallen leaves. If I hadn't followed her visually all the way to that spot, I doubt that I could have picked her out from the surrounding woods.

I stayed inside the truck and sketched the deer's beautiful face and watching eyes. Then I drew her body. The deer remained in one position for a long while. I had time to add some muscling and shading to her figure. She flicked her tail, flashing its pure white underside, and swiveled one of her ears around to pick up some sound behind her. I added both movements to my sketch.

I used binoculars to see the deer close-up as I sketched her figure and facial features. Then, looking at the deer with my eyes alone, I added her body coloration, musculature, and shading.

To make an animal look camouflaged, use the same tonal values of gray on the surrounding scenery as you used on the animal.

I sketched only the deer for as long as she remained in view. After she had gone, I set up my easel in the open air and completed the scene, adding the autumn woods around my sketch of the deer.

I used binoculars to see the nearest geese as I sketched them. When I was sketching faraway geese, I looked only with my eyes. With my naked eyes it was easier to reduce the distant birds to their essential forms and markings.

When you are sketching geese from life, notice how geese in a group tend to land in unison, all gliding down slowly, each bird assuming the same flight attitude. On the other hand, when geese are taking off in a group, each goose flaps its wings at its own rate.

On a family trip west to spend a few days in the Adirondacks, we saw thousands of Canada geese congregating in a broad, flat Champlain Valley meadow. We could linger only a few minutes to enjoy the spectacle before we had to continue onward to our destination.

On our way back home, I pulled off the road and parked near the meadow full of geese. We spent all that afternoon watching, listening to, and sketching the wild geese.

I approached the birds very slowly. When I was about a couple of hundred feet away from them, I crouched, rested my sketch pad on the barbed wire of some old and rotting fencing, and sketched the closest pair of geese. It was very windy, and my paper kept blowing up into my face. I think it was that flashing of white paper that alerted one of the geese I was sketching. It stretched its neck long and tall and cast a wary eye back in my direction.

The strong wind blowing over the meadow seemed to make all the geese nervous. Every once in a while a whole section of birds suddenly took off together, flew a short distance, and settled down in unison on some new place.

I sketched the two geese for only as long as they remained where they were. When their group took flight, I went back to the car and rejoined my family.

To sketch each goose, I began by outlining its body shape, including its neck and head. Then I sketched in the eye and bill detail. I added feathers and body markings last.

Canada Geese
drawn from life
McAyne
Oct 1987

Beech Woods
Jim Arnosky 1987

Back home in the mountains I found a wooded ridge about half a mile long that is dominated by beech trees. Most of the beeches have been climbed by bears. There are claw marks in the trees' smooth, silver-gray bark. Every autumn bears come here to gorge on ripened beechnuts. Bear claw marks from previous years have become blackened scars. Recently made claw marks cut through the bark, showing the white beech wood underneath.

On a sunny but very cold October morning I carried my easel up the steep ridge to a place where, on an earlier expedition, I had discovered a group of large, extensively clawed beech trees. Once there, I noticed a broad space on the ground that had been brushed clear of fallen leaves, where a bear had recently sprawled. On that spot I set up my easel, extending its legs so I could stand tall to sketch the magnificent, clawed trees and breathe deeply the air bears breathe.

It seemed appropriate to use my big, broad-pointed carpenter's pencil to sketch this scene.

To sketch the claw marks in the trees, I dug at the paper with the pencil point, just as a bear's claw would dig into bark.

The smooth texture created by soft pencil lead on my drawing paper nearly duplicated that of the smooth-barked trees.

When you are sketching woodland, don't be afraid to overlap and crisscross lines, the way twigs and branches appear to overlap and crisscross in the actual woods.

Beechnuts grow high on the terminal twigs and branches of a beech tree's crown. A bear climbs up, stations itself near the strong center trunk, and, by pulling and bending the outer branches inward, brings the nuts within reach. Many branches are snapped and broken. The bear squashes down the bent and broken branches and sits or stands upon them while feeding.

After a while a mat of broken branches forms in the tree. These matted-down leaves and branches look like huge nests. The copper-colored beech leaves cling to the broken branches long after the rest of the beech leaves have fallen. Then the matted areas of broken, leafy branches are most conspicuous.

This particular beech tree has a number of "bear nests" in it. The largest, at the tree's top, is approximately eight feet in diameter.

When sketching trees, pay close attention to the clear spots of light that shine through the branches and leaves. As you work, use your eraser to keep those spots in your sketch clean and white.

To draw broken branches, "break" your lines.

After sketching and shading in the leafy masses, I formed the tip of my kneadable eraser into the shape of a tiny beach leaf, and used it to lift out light-colored leaves from the darkest areas.

Bear Tree
JEA 1987

37

Early in November, on a day as crisp and cool as an apple, I set my easel in a friend's small orchard. The trees' leaves were gone, and so were many of the apples. One tree had a good many yellow apples still clinging to its branches. That was the tree I had come to sketch.

All around the orchard, deer tracks were pressed into the ground. Deer had been coming regularly to eat the low-hanging or windfall fruit.

I sketched throughout the afternoon and lingered after sunset, hoping to glimpse a deer. However, without the sunlight, the air quickly turned from cool to cold, and I was not dressed warmly enough. Shivering, I packed up and headed home.

I began by sketching the tree's trunk and main limbs. Then, by scribbling, scraping, and scratching lines onto my paper, I matched the tree's tangle of branches and twigs.

I stepped back often to view my work from a distance so I could make sure the lines of the sketch were resembling those of the apple tree.

To make my apples look dense, like the real apples, I added a little shading to every sphere I created. Then I underscored each apple in the sketch with a heavyweight line to make it look as though it was hanging, ready to drop.

We had some snow mixed with freezing rain, after which the weather was bitterly cold. I revisited the cornfield. Its corn hadn't yet been harvested. The stalks were pale and brittle. The sound of their long leaves tapping together in the wind reminded me of old bones cracking. The tops of the stalks drooped. Their tassels looked spent. The ears of corn were all hanging downward, and each ear had a brown beard of dry cornsilk.

November Corn
rain and snow
J Sel 1987

In another of the farmer's cornfields, nearer to a village, the corn had been recently cut. This was one of the ears the machinery had missed. Half of the corn kernels had been knocked off and scattered—golden nuggets that would be found later by prospecting wildlife.

As I sketched, I heard sounds of country life. Crows were calling from a nearby field. The village church bell rang on the hour. A passing freight train whistled. There were also the gunshots of local hunters firing their rifles, sighting them in, getting ready for deer season.

A male deer develops antlers on the crown of its head. The base of an antler is called the pedicel. From the pedicel grows the antler's main beam. Antler tines or "points," if there are any, emanate from the main beam.

Antlers are easier to draw if you begin with the pedicel, sketch in the main beam, and then add the tines.

Every November, during deer hunting season, I study, measure, and sketch deer that have been killed. I do this to learn more about animal anatomy and to gain understanding of individual animals' lives.

6 point in antlers
1 sheared off
during rutting

Jim Arnosky Nov 1987
(176 lbs live weight)

141 lbs dressed
killed Oct 2nd

43

Whenever you are drawing deer, think of these dimensions: An average white-tailed deer measures three feet in height at its shoulders and five feet in length from the tip of its nose to the root of its tail. It weighs approximately 150 pounds. The deer you see in these sketches was larger than average.

I've outlined the major muscle areas in a deer's body. Look for them when you are sketching deer from life.

Whitetailed Deer
172½ lbs field dressed
(approx. 216 lbs live weight)

measured 22½ inches around neck

antlers - 8 points
a ninth point lost - might have been damaged in velvet during summer.

Nov. 87

length of body to tip of tail from nose 73 inches

hair on forehead - long and coarse

eye in detail
(actual size)

A deer eye is dark and there is no distinct pupil.

Always reserve your deepest, darkest blacks for the lightless places in the scene you are sketching, such as holes or crevices.

By carefully drawing the fallen leaves in their proper proportion to the scene, I've conveyed the enormous size of the boulders.

Autumn is ending. Soon the bears will be denning up. If I were a bear, I'd choose the crevice between these massive boulders as my winter den. The crevice opening faces north, so it would stay a constant cold, lessening the danger of being iced in by melting snow. The site is surrounded by tree-covered mountains. It is a silent and peaceful place to sleep away the winter days. Close by is a spring, bubbling up through the ground, for that thirsty first drink come April.

But I am not a bear. Long johns and woolen clothing are not as warm as a thick layering of fat and fur. The longer I stood sketching this scene, the colder I felt. A northern wind chilled the back of my neck. My nose turned cherry red, and the air smelled like snow.

Nov. 1987
— A last long look at
the forest floor
before snow.